February 2024

SUNDAY	MONDAY	TUESDAY	WEDNESDAY
28	29	30	31
4	5	6	7
11 eat Bfast.	12	13	14 eat Bfast. Ash Wednesday, Lent begins Valentine's Day
18	19	20	21
25	26 Presidents' Day	27	28

Handwritten notes: 8, 9, 10, 11, 15, 16, 17, 3 DAY 116, 18, 22, 23, 24, 25

● NEW MOON ◑ FIRST QUARTER ○ FULL MOON ◐ LAST QUARTER

THURSDAY	FRIDAY	SATURDAY
1	◑ 6:18 pm EST 2	3
5	6 Groundhog Day	7
8	● 5:59 pm EST 9	10
12	13	14
15	◐ 10:01 am EST 16	17
19 Flag Day (Canada)	20	21
22	23	○ 7:30 am EST 24
29	1	

february

Imbolc

February

Groundhog Day | ◑ 6:18 pm EST

MONDAY

5

_____

_____

_____

_____

_____

_____

TUESDAY

6

_____

_____

_____

_____

Waitangi Day (New Zealand)

WEDNESDAY

7

_____

_____

_____

_____

_____

THURSDAY

8

FRIDAY

9

● 5:59 pm EST

SATURDAY

10

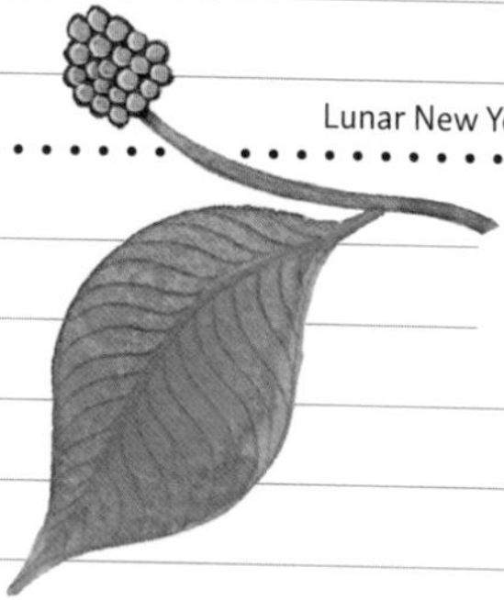

Lunar New Year (Dragon)

SUNDAY

11

FEBRUARY 2024

MONDAY

12

TUESDAY

13

Mardi Gras

WEDNESDAY

14

Ash Wednesday, Lent begins | Valentine's Day

THURSDAY

15

Flag Day (Canada)

FRIDAY

16

◔ 10:01 am EST

SATURDAY

17

Random Acts of Kindness Day

SUNDAY

18

February 2024

MONDAY
19

Presidents' Day

TUESDAY
20

WEDNESDAY
21

THURSDAY

22

FRIDAY

23

SATURDAY

24

○ 7:30 am EST

SUNDAY

25

February 2024

MONDAY
26

TUESDAY
27

WEDNESDAY
28

Leap Day

March 2024

SUNDAY	MONDAY	TUESDAY	WEDNESDAY
25	26	27	28
☽ 10:24 am EST 3	4	5	6
● 5:00 am EDT 10	11	12	13
Daylight Saving Time begins Ramadan begins at sunset			
☽ 12:11 am EDT 17	18	19	20
St. Patrick's Day		Spring Equinox	
24	○ 3:00 am EDT 25	26	27
31 British Summer Time begins (UK) Easter			

THURSDAY	FRIDAY	SATURDAY	
29	1	2	_____
			_____
			_____
			_____
7	8	9	_____
14	15	16	
21	22	23	
28	29	30	
	Good Friday		

March

March 2024

FRIDAY

1

SATURDAY

2

SUNDAY

3

◑ 10:24 am EST

MARCH 2024

MONDAY
4

TUESDAY
5

WEDNESDAY
6

International Women's Day

March

Daylight Saving Time begins | Mother's Day (UK) | Ramadan begins at sunset | ● 5:00 am EDT

MARCH 2024

MONDAY

11

TUESDAY

12

WEDNESDAY

13

March

St. Patrick's Day | ☽ 12:11 am EDT

MONDAY

18

TUESDAY

19

Spring Equinox 11:06 pm EDT

WEDNESDAY

20

THURSDAY

21

FRIDAY

22

SATURDAY

23

March

SUNDAY

24

MarCH 2024

MONDAY

25

Penumbral lunar eclipse 3:13 am EDT | ○ 3:00 am EDT

TUESDAY

26

WEDNESDAY

27

Good Friday

March

British Summer Time begins (UK) | Easter

APRIL 2024

SUNDAY	MONDAY	TUESDAY	WEDNESDAY
31	◑ 11:15 pm EDT 1 April Fools' Day Easter Monday (Australia, Canada, UK)	2	3
7	● 2:21 pm EDT 8	9 Eid al-Fitr begins at sunset	10
14	◐ 3:13 pm EDT 15	16	17
21	22 Earth Day Passover begins at sunset	○ 7:49 pm EDT 23	24
28	29	30	1

● NEW MOON ◐ FIRST QUARTER ○ FULL MOON ◑ LAST QUARTER

THURSDAY	FRIDAY	SATURDAY
4	5	6
11	12	13
18	19	20
25	26	27
ANZAC Day (Australia, New Zealand)		
2	3	4

April

MONDAY

1

April Fools' Day | Easter Monday (Australia, Canada, UK)
Mercury retrograde until April 25 | ◑ 11:15 pm EDT

TUESDAY

2

WEDNESDAY

3

MONDAY

8

Total solar eclipse 2:17 pm EDT | ● 2:21 pm EDT

TUESDAY

9

Eid al-Fitr begins at sunset

WEDNESDAY

10

THURSDAY

11

FRIDAY

12

SATURDAY

13

SUNDAY

14

APRIL

APRIL 2024

MONDAY

15

● 3:13 pm EDT

TUESDAY

16

WEDNESDAY

17

April

APRIL 2024

MONDAY

22

Earth Day | Passover begins at sunset

TUESDAY

23

○ 7:49 pm EDT

WEDNESDAY

24

THURSDAY

25

ANZAC Day (Australia, New Zealand)

FRIDAY

26

Arbor Day

SATURDAY

27

SUNDAY

28

April

APRIL 2024

MONDAY
29

TUESDAY
30

MAY 2024

SUNDAY	MONDAY	TUESDAY	WEDNESDAY
28	29	30	● 7:27 am EDT 1
5	6	● 11:22 pm EDT 7	8
	Early May Bank Holiday (UK)		
12	13	14	◐ 7:48 am EDT 15
Mother's Day			
19	20	21	22
		Victoria Day (Canada, Scotland)	
26	27	28	29
	Memorial Day Spring Bank Holiday (UK)		

● NEW MOON ◑ FIRST QUARTER ○ FULL MOON ◐ LAST QUARTER

2	3	4
9	10	11
16	17	18
○ 9:53 am EDT 23	24	25
◑ 1:13 pm EDT 30	31	

May

MAY 2024

WEDNESDAY

1

Beltane | May Day | ◑ 7:27 am EDT

FRIDAY

3

SATURDAY

4

SUNDAY

5

Cinco de Mayo | Pascha

MAY 2024

MONDAY

6

Early May Bank Holiday (UK)

TUESDAY

7

● 11:22 pm EDT

WEDNESDAY

8

Mother's Day

MAY 2024

MONDAY

13

TUESDAY

14

WEDNESDAY

15

◐ 7:48 am EDT

FRIDAY

17

Bike to Work Day

SATURDAY

18

Armed Forces Day

SUNDAY

19

MONDAY

20

Victoria Day (Canada, Scotland)

TUESDAY

21

WEDNESDAY

22

Vesak | ○ 9:53 am EDT

MONDAY

27

Memorial Day | Spring Bank Holiday (UK)

TUESDAY

28

WEDNESDAY

29

◑ 1:13 pm EDT

JUNE 2024

SUNDAY	MONDAY	TUESDAY	WEDNESDAY
26	27	28	29
2	3	4	5
9	10	11	12
16	17	18	19
23 Eid al-Adha begins at sunset Father's Day	24	25	26 Juneteenth
30			

● NEW MOON ☽ FIRST QUARTER ○ FULL MOON ☾ LAST QUARTER

THURSDAY	FRIDAY	SATURDAY
30	31	1
● 8:38 am EDT 6	7	8
13	◑ 1:18 am EDT 14	15
	Flag Day	
20	○ 9:08 pm EDT 21	22
Summer Solstice		
27	◐ 5:53 pm EDT 28	29

june

JUNE 2024

SATURDAY

1

SUNDAY

2

MONDAY

3

TUESDAY

4

WEDNESDAY

5

World Environment Day

THURSDAY

6

● 8:38 am EDT

FRIDAY

7

SATURDAY

8

SUNDAY

9

JUNE 2024

MONDAY

10

TUESDAY

11

Shavuot begins at sunset

WEDNESDAY

12

june

Flag Day | ◐ 1:18 am EDT

Eid al-Adha begins at sunset | Father's Day

JUNE 2024

MONDAY

17

TUESDAY

18

WEDNESDAY

19

Juneteenth

20

Summer Solstice 4:51 pm EDT | World Refugee Day

21

June

○ 9:08 pm EDT

22

23

JUNE 2024

MONDAY

24

TUESDAY

25

WEDNESDAY

26

27

28

◐ 5:53 pm EDT

29

30

JULY 2024

SUNDAY	MONDAY	TUESDAY	WEDNESDAY
30	1	2	3
	Canada Day		
7	8	9	10
14	15	16	17
○ 6:17 am EDT 21	22	23	24
28	29	30	31

● NEW MOON ◑ FIRST QUARTER ○ FULL MOON ◑ LAST QUARTER

THURSDAY	FRIDAY	SATURDAY
4	● 6:57 pm EDT 5	6
Independence Day		Muharram begins at sunset
11	12	◑ 6:49 pm EDT 13
	Orangemen's Day (Northern Ireland)	
18	19	20
25	26	◑ 10:52 pm EDT 27
1	2	

JULY

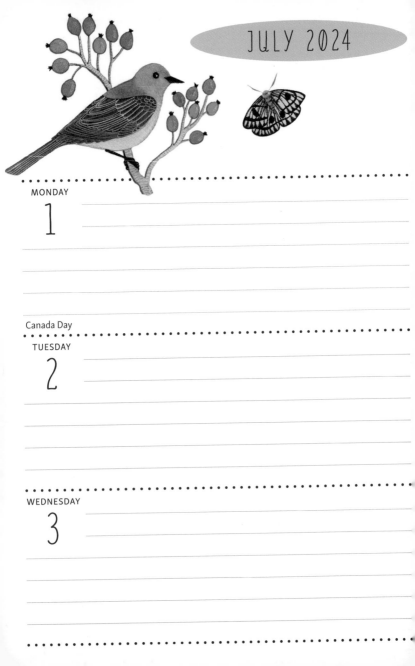

MONDAY

1

Canada Day

TUESDAY

2

WEDNESDAY

3

4

Independence Day

5

● 6:57 pm EDT

6

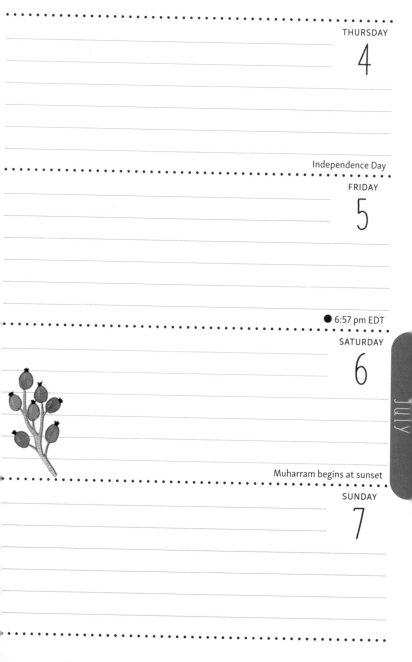

JULY

Muharram begins at sunset

7

JULY 2024

MONDAY
8

TUESDAY
9

WEDNESDAY
10

Orangemen's Day (Northern Ireland)

◐ 6:49 pm EDT

JULY 2024

MONDAY
15

TUESDAY
16

WEDNESDAY
17

JULY

○ 6:17 am EDT

JULY 2024

MONDAY
22

TUESDAY
23

WEDNESDAY
24

THURSDAY

25

FRIDAY

26

SATURDAY

27

JULY

◑ 10:52 pm EDT

SUNDAY

28

MONDAY

29

TUESDAY

30

WEDNESDAY

31

AUGUST 2024

SUNDAY	MONDAY	TUESDAY	WEDNESDAY
28	29	30	31
● 7:13 am EDT 4	5	6	7
	August Bank Holiday (Scotland) Civic Holiday (Canada)		
11	◑ 11:19 am EDT 12	13	14
18	○ 2:26 pm EDT 19	20	21
25	◐ 5:26 am EDT 26	27	28
	Summer Bank Holiday (UK)		

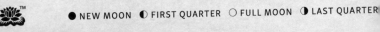

● NEW MOON ◑ FIRST QUARTER ○ FULL MOON ◐ LAST QUARTER

THURSDAY	FRIDAY	SATURDAY
1	2	3
8	9	10
15	16	17
22	23	24
29	30	31

August

Lughnasadh

August

Mercury retrograde until August 28 | ● 7:13 am EDT

MONDAY

5

August Bank Holiday (Scotland) | Civic Holiday (Canada)

TUESDAY

6

WEDNESDAY

7

THURSDAY

8

FRIDAY

9

SATURDAY

10

SUNDAY

11

MONDAY

12

◗ 11:19 am EDT

TUESDAY

13

WEDNESDAY

14

MONDAY

19

○ 2:26 pm EDT

TUESDAY

20

WEDNESDAY

21

FRIDAY

23

SATURDAY

24

SUNDAY

25

August

MONDAY

26

Summer Bank Holiday (UK) | Women's Equality Day | ◑ 5:26 am EDT

TUESDAY

27

WEDNESDAY

28

september 2024

SUNDAY	MONDAY	TUESDAY	WEDNESDAY
1	● 9:55 pm EDT 2	3	4
	Labor Day (USA, Canada)		
8	9	10	◑ 2:06 am EDT 11
15	16	○ 10:34 pm EDT 17	18
22	23	◑ 2:50 pm EDT 24	25
Autumnal Equinox 29	30	1	2
	National Day for Truth and Reconciliation (Canada)		

● NEW MOON   ◐ FIRST QUARTER   ○ FULL MOON   ◑ LAST QUARTER

THURSDAY	FRIDAY	SATURDAY
5	6	7
12	13	14
19	20	21
26	27	28
3	4	

September 2024

SUNDAY

1

September 2024

MONDAY

2

Labor Day (USA, Canada) | ● 9:55 pm EDT

TUESDAY

3

WEDNESDAY

4

Grandparents Day

September 2024

MONDAY
9

TUESDAY
10

WEDNESDAY
11

Patriot Day | ◐ 2:06 am EDT

THURSDAY

12

FRIDAY

13

SATURDAY

14

SUNDAY

15

MONDAY

16

TUESDAY

17

Partial lunar eclipse 10:44 pm EDT | ○ 10:34 pm EDT

WEDNESDAY

18

THURSDAY

19

FRIDAY

20

SATURDAY

21

International Day of Peace

SUNDAY

22

Autumnal Equinox 8:44 am EDT

MONDAY

23

TUESDAY

24

◑ 2:50 pm EDT

WEDNESDAY

25

THURSDAY

26

FRIDAY

27

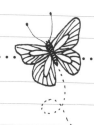

SATURDAY

28

SUNDAY

29

september 2024

MONDAY

30

National Day for Truth and Reconciliation (Canada)

OCTOBER 2024

SUNDAY	MONDAY	TUESDAY	WEDNESDAY
29	30	1	2 ● 2:49 pm EDT
			Rosh Hashanah begins at sunset
6	7	8	9
13	14	15	16
	Columbus Day Indigenous Peoples Day Thanksgiving (Canada)		
20	21	22	23
27	28	29	30
British Summer Time ends (UK)			

● NEW MOON ◐ FIRST QUARTER ○ FULL MOON ◑ LAST QUARTER

THURSDAY	FRIDAY	SATURDAY
3	4	5
◑ 2:55 pm EDT 10	11	12
	Yom Kippur begins at sunset	
○ 7:26 am EDT 17	18	19
◐ 4:03 am EDT 24	25	26
31	1	2
Halloween		

OCTOBER 2024

TUESDAY

1

WEDNESDAY

2

Annular solar eclipse 2:45 pm EDT | Rosh Hashanah begins at sunset | ● 2:49 pm EDT

OCTOBER

OCTOBER 2024

MONDAY

7

TUESDAY

8

WEDNESDAY

9

THURSDAY

10

◗ 2:55 pm EDT

FRIDAY

11

Yom Kippur begins at sunset

SATURDAY

12

SUNDAY

13

OCTOBER 2024

MONDAY

14

Columbus Day | Indigenous Peoples Day | Thanksgiving (Canada)

TUESDAY

15

WEDNESDAY

16

Sukkot begins at sunset

○ 7:26 am EDT

october

OCTOBER 2024

MONDAY
21

TUESDAY
22

WEDNESDAY
23

United Nations Day | ◑ 4:03 am EDT

OCTOBER

British Summer Time ends (UK)

MONDAY

28

TUESDAY

29

WEDNESDAY

30

Halloween | Samhain

NOVEMBER 2024

SUNDAY	MONDAY	TUESDAY	WEDNESDAY
27	28	29	30
3 Daylight Saving Time ends	4	5 Election Day	6
10	11 Remembrance Day (Australia, Canada, UK) Veterans Day	12	13
17	18	19	20
24	25	26	27

● NEW MOON ◑ FIRST QUARTER ○ FULL MOON ◐ LAST QUARTER

THURSDAY	FRIDAY	SATURDAY	
31	● 8:47 am EDT 1	2	_____
			_____
			_____
			_____
			_____
7	8	◐ 12:56 am EST 9	_____
14 ○ 4:29 pm EST	15	16	
21 ◑ 8:28 pm EST	22	23	
28	29	30	
Thanksgiving		St. Andrew's Day (Scotland)	

November

NOVEMBER 2024

FRIDAY

1

Diwali | ● 8:47 am EDT

SATURDAY

2

November

SUNDAY

3

Daylight Saving Time ends

November 2024

MONDAY

4

TUESDAY

5

Election Day

WEDNESDAY

6

THURSDAY

7

FRIDAY

8

SATURDAY

9

November

◐ 12:56 am EST

SUNDAY

10

NOVEMBER 2024

MONDAY

11

Remembrance Day (Australia, Canada, UK) | Veterans Day

TUESDAY

12

WEDNESDAY

13

FRIDAY

15

○ 4:29 pm EST

SATURDAY

16

SUNDAY

17

MONDAY

18

TUESDAY

19

WEDNESDAY

20

◑ 8:28 pm EST

November

NOVEMBER 2024

MONDAY

25

Mercury retrograde until December 15

TUESDAY

26

WEDNESDAY

27

THURSDAY

28

Thanksgiving

FRIDAY

29

SATURDAY

30

November

St. Andrew's Day (Scotland)

December 2024

SUNDAY	MONDAY	TUESDAY	WEDNESDAY
● 1:21 am EST 1	2	3	4
◑ 10:27 am EST 8	9	10	11
○ 4:02 am EST 15	16	17	18
◗ 5:18 pm EST 22	23	24	25 Christmas Hanukkah begins at sunset
29	● 5:27 pm EST 30	31 New Year's Eve	1

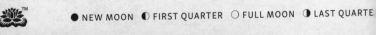

● NEW MOON ◑ FIRST QUARTER ○ FULL MOON ◗ LAST QUARTER

THURSDAY	FRIDAY	SATURDAY
5	6	7
12	13	14
19	20	21
26	27	Winter Solstice 28
Boxing Day (Australia, Canada, UK) Kwanzaa begins 2	3	4

December

DECEMBER 2024

Advent begins | ● 1:21 am EST

December 2024

MONDAY

2

TUESDAY

3

WEDNESDAY

4

Pearl Harbor Remembrance Day

December

◑ 10:27 am EST

MONDAY

9

TUESDAY

10

Human Rights Day

WEDNESDAY

11

December

○ 4:02 am EST

MONDAY

16

TUESDAY

17

WEDNESDAY

18

THURSDAY
19

FRIDAY
20

SATURDAY
21

Winter Solstice 4:20 am EST

SUNDAY
22

◑ 5:18 pm EST

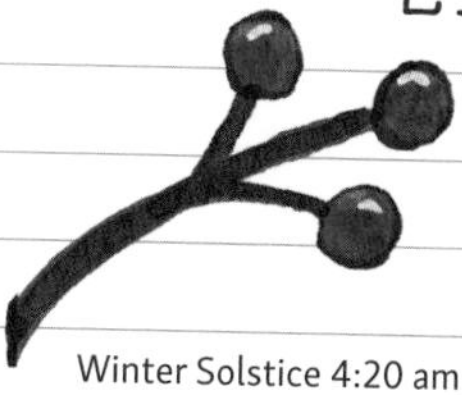

MONDAY

23

_____

TUESDAY

24

_____

WEDNESDAY

25

_____

Christmas | Hanukkah begins at sunset

THURSDAY

26

Boxing Day (Australia, Canada, UK) | Kwanzaa begins

FRIDAY

27

SATURDAY

28

SUNDAY

29

december

DeCEMBER 2024

MONDAY

30

● 5:27 pm EST

TUESDAY

31

New Year's Eve

January 2025

SUNDAY	MONDAY	TUESDAY	WEDNESDAY
29	30	31	1
			New Year's Day
5	6 ◗ 6:56 pm EST	7	8
12	13 ○ 5:27 pm EST	14	15
19	20 ◑ 3:31 pm EST	21	22
	Martin Luther King Jr. Day		
26	27	28	29 ● 7:36 am EST
Australia Day			

● NEW MOON ◗ FIRST QUARTER ○ FULL MOON ◑ LAST QUARTE

THURSDAY	FRIDAY	SATURDAY
2	3	4
9	10	11
16	17	18
23	24	25
30	31	

WEDNESDAY

1

New Year's Day

FRIDAY

3

SATURDAY

4

SUNDAY

5

January 2025

MONDAY

6

◑ 6:56 pm EST

TUESDAY

7

WEDNESDAY

8

THURSDAY

9

FRIDAY

10

SATURDAY

11

SUNDAY

12

JANUARY 2025

MONDAY

13

○ 5:27 pm EST

TUESDAY

14

WEDNESDAY

15

THURSDAY

16

FRIDAY

17

SATURDAY

18

SUNDAY

19

MONDAY

20

Martin Luther King Jr. Day

TUESDAY

21

◑ 3:31 pm EST

WEDNESDAY

22

THURSDAY

23

FRIDAY

24

SATURDAY

25

SUNDAY

26

Australia Day

MONDAY

27

TUESDAY

28

WEDNESDAY

29

Lunar New Year (Snake) | ● 7:36 am EST

CONTACTS

NAME

ADDRESS

PHONE

EMAIL

NAME

ADDRESS

PHONE

EMAIL

NAME

ADDRESS

PHONE

EMAIL

NAME

ADDRESS

PHONE

EMAIL

NAME

ADDRESS

PHONE

EMAIL

CONTACTS

NAME

ADDRESS

PHONE

EMAIL

NAME

ADDRESS

PHONE

EMAIL

NAME

ADDRESS

PHONE

EMAIL

NAME

ADDRESS

PHONE

EMAIL

NAME

ADDRESS

PHONE

EMAIL

BIRTHDAYS & OCCASIONS

JANUARY

FEBRUARY

MARCH

APRIL

MAY

JUNE

BIRTHDAYS & OCCASIONS

JULY

AUGUST

SEPTEMBER

OCTOBER

NOVEMBER

DECEMBER

HABIT TRACKER

MONTH:

HABIT:

① ② ③ ④ ⑤ ⑥ ⑦ ⑧ ⑨ ⑩ ⑪
⑫ ⑬ ⑭ ⑮ ⑯ ⑰ ⑱ ⑲ ⑳ ㉑ ㉒
㉓ ㉔ ㉕ ㉖ ㉗ ㉘ ㉙ ㉚ ㉛

GOAL: **REWARD:**

MONTH:

HABIT:

① ② ③ ④ ⑤ ⑥ ⑦ ⑧ ⑨ ⑩ ⑪
⑫ ⑬ ⑭ ⑮ ⑯ ⑰ ⑱ ⑲ ⑳ ㉑ ㉒
㉓ ㉔ ㉕ ㉖ ㉗ ㉘ ㉙ ㉚ ㉛

GOAL: **REWARD:**

MONTH:

HABIT:

① ② ③ ④ ⑤ ⑥ ⑦ ⑧ ⑨ ⑩ ⑪
⑫ ⑬ ⑭ ⑮ ⑯ ⑰ ⑱ ⑲ ⑳ ㉑ ㉒
㉓ ㉔ ㉕ ㉖ ㉗ ㉘ ㉙ ㉚ ㉛

GOAL: **REWARD:**

HABIT TRACKER

MONTH:

HABIT:

(1) (2) (3) (4) (5) (6) (7) (8) (9) (10) (11)

(12) (13) (14) (15) (16) (17) (18) (19) (20) (21) (22)

(23) (24) (25) (26) (27) (28) (29) (30) (31)

GOAL: **REWARD:**

MONTH:

HABIT:

(1) (2) (3) (4) (5) (6) (7) (8) (9) (10) (11)

(12) (13) (14) (15) (16) (17) (18) (19) (20) (21) (22)

(23) (24) (25) (26) (27) (28) (29) (30) (31)

GOAL: **REWARD:**

MONTH:

HABIT:

(1) (2) (3) (4) (5) (6) (7) (8) (9) (10) (11)

(12) (13) (14) (15) (16) (17) (18) (19) (20) (21) (22)

(23) (24) (25) (26) (27) (28) (29) (30) (31)

GOAL: **REWARD:**

HABIT TRACKER

MONTH:

HABIT:

(1) (2) (3) (4) (5) (6) (7) (8) (9) (10) (11)

(12) (13) (14) (15) (16) (17) (18) (19) (20) (21) (22)

(23) (24) (25) (26) (27) (28) (29) (30) (31)

GOAL: **REWARD:**

MONTH:

HABIT:

(1) (2) (3) (4) (5) (6) (7) (8) (9) (10) (11)

(12) (13) (14) (15) (16) (17) (18) (19) (20) (21) (22)

(23) (24) (25) (26) (27) (28) (29) (30) (31)

GOAL: **REWARD:**

MONTH:

HABIT:

(1) (2) (3) (4) (5) (6) (7) (8) (9) (10) (11)

(12) (13) (14) (15) (16) (17) (18) (19) (20) (21) (22)

(23) (24) (25) (26) (27) (28) (29) (30) (31)

GOAL: **REWARD:**

HABIT TRACKER

MONTH:

HABIT:

(1) (2) (3) (4) (5) (6) (7) (8) (9) (10) (11)
(12) (13) (14) (15) (16) (17) (18) (19) (20) (21) (22)
(23) (24) (25) (26) (27) (28) (29) (30) (31)

GOAL: **REWARD:**

MONTH:

HABIT:

(1) (2) (3) (4) (5) (6) (7) (8) (9) (10) (11)
(12) (13) (14) (15) (16) (17) (18) (19) (20) (21) (22)
(23) (24) (25) (26) (27) (28) (29) (30) (31)

GOAL: **REWARD:**

MONTH:

HABIT:

(1) (2) (3) (4) (5) (6) (7) (8) (9) (10) (11)
(12) (13) (14) (15) (16) (17) (18) (19) (20) (21) (22)
(23) (24) (25) (26) (27) (28) (29) (30) (31)

GOAL: **REWARD:**

2025 AT A GLANCE

JANUARY 2025

S	M	T	W	T	F	S
			1	2	3	4
5	6	7	8	9	10	11
12	13	14	15	16	17	18
19	20	21	22	23	24	25
26	27	28	29	30	31	

FEBRUARY 2025

S	M	T	W	T	F	S
						1
2	3	4	5	6	7	8
9	10	11	12	13	14	15
16	17	18	19	20	21	22
23	24	25	26	27	28	

MARCH 2025

S	M	T	W	T	F	S
						1
2	3	4	5	6	7	8
9	10	11	12	13	14	15
16	17	18	19	20	21	22
23	24	25	26	27	28	29
30	31					

APRIL 2025

S	M	T	W	T	F	S
		1	2	3	4	5
6	7	8	9	10	11	12
13	14	15	16	17	18	19
20	21	22	23	24	25	26
27	28	29	30			

MAY 2025

S	M	T	W	T	F	S
				1	2	3
4	5	6	7	8	9	10
11	12	13	14	15	16	17
18	19	20	21	22	23	24
25	26	27	28	29	30	31

JUNE 2025

S	M	T	W	T	F	S
1	2	3	4	5	6	7
8	9	10	11	12	13	14
15	16	17	18	19	20	21
22	23	24	25	26	27	28
29	30					

JULY 2025

S	M	T	W	T	F	S
		1	2	3	4	5
6	7	8	9	10	11	12
13	14	15	16	17	18	19
20	21	22	23	24	25	26
27	28	29	30	31		

AUGUST 2025

S	M	T	W	T	F	S
					1	2
3	4	5	6	7	8	9
10	11	12	13	14	15	16
17	18	19	20	21	22	23
24	25	26	27	28	29	30
31						

SEPTEMBER 2025

S	M	T	W	T	F	S
	1	2	3	4	5	6
7	8	9	10	11	12	13
14	15	16	17	18	19	20
21	22	23	24	25	26	27
28	29	30				

OCTOBER 2025

S	M	T	W	T	F	S
			1	2	3	4
5	6	7	8	9	10	11
12	13	14	15	16	17	18
19	20	21	22	23	24	25
26	27	28	29	30	31	

NOVEMBER 2025

S	M	T	W	T	F	S
						1
2	3	4	5	6	7	8
9	10	11	12	13	14	15
16	17	18	19	20	21	22
23	24	25	26	27	28	29
30						

DECEMBER 2025

S	M	T	W	T	F	S
	1	2	3	4	5	6
7	8	9	10	11	12	13
14	15	16	17	18	19	20
21	22	23	24	25	26	27
28	29	30	31			